The $18 Entrepreneur

The $18 Entrepreneur

DEDICATION

This book is dedicated to **Mrs. Jeannette Mack** and **Mrs. Linda Saulsberry**, two powerful and positive women who have stood by their men. For as long as we can both remember Bill and I have chased the Network dream. We have had some successes and many failures. To finally find a dream business that allows the average person to accomplish above average results is awesome.

In the process of seeking out new opportunities Both Bill and Myself have subjected Jeannette and Linda to an untold number of meetings, new ventures and exposure to a plethora of products that we believed in and all too often they ended up a bust.

Through it all both of these **superhero spouses** have been the support, the sounding board, and the guinea pigs to products, services and just plain nonsense.

It is with this background that we launch: The $18 Entrepreneur.

COPYRIGHT PAGE

Published   Self Published Authors Network

A product of SPAN Books: Dallas Texas

Quantity discounts are available on bulk purchases of this book

ACKNOWLEDGEMENTS

We would like to acknowledge all the leaders and readers who are seeking and living the American dream. The direct sales industry has given more people more opportunity than any other single entity. We are grateful to life in a country that allows you to dream and pursue that dream. More importantly to be able to reach it based on your efforts and actions.

The $18 Entrepreneur

CONTENTS

Dedication	3
Copyright page	4
Acknowledgements	5
Why We Wrote this Book:	7
Chapter 1	8
The philosophy behind The $18 Entrepreneur	8
Chapter 2.	12
"Network Marketing isn't perfect, it's just better	12
Chapter 3	14
What Next?	14
Chapter 4	16
The $18 Entrepreneur Elephant Eating Experience:	16
Chapter 5	18
Eighteen Steps to engagement~	18
CHAPTER 6	42
First Sponsored Partner—*What do I do?*	42
Chapter 7	46
Reference Material	46

WHY WE WROTE THIS BOOK:

Families today have found themselves fretting about exactly what the future holds. Many families also live paycheck to paycheck.

If you are like the majority of us in the working world, you might have considered beginning a home based business. You might have wondered what it will take to start.

You may have even weighed the pros and cons of an online business vs a MLM business. Do one of these simple situations look familiar? Would you like to change it?

 "The $18 Entrepreneur" will guide you through the steps to achieving your goals. No need to buckle up, the ride will be smooth. Welcome to the "TEAM".

CHAPTER 1

THE PHILOSOPHY BEHIND THE $18 ENTREPRENEUR

Who is the prototypical American Millionaire? What would he/she tell you about themselves? * Taken from the book- "The Millionaire Next Door"

- I am a fifty-seven-year-old male/female, married with three children. About 70 percent of us earn 80 percent or more of our household's income.
- About one in five of us are retired. About two-thirds of us, who are working, are self-employed. *Interestingly, self-employed people make up less than 20 percent of the workers in America but account for two-thirds of the millionaires.* In addition, three out of four of us who are **self-employed** consider ourselves Entrepreneurs.

- As a group, we believe that education is extremely important for our children, their children, and ourselves. We spend heavily for the educations of our offspring. Does this sound like you, earning more than 80 percent of the people you know? Self-employed with income greater than 98 percent of the population? Are you working 40 hours per week with time to spend with family? Can you miss a month of work and still have money coming in? Do you own your business or does the business own you?

The rest of this book was designed to help you earn like 2 percent of the country and have the time freedom to enjoy it. It was designed to educate you while allowing you the opportunity to give to the people you care the most about. If I were to draw a line and tell you that simply stepping over it would change your life and make you the next millionaire, would you take that step? Certainly, you would. If you knew that taking that step would guarantee riches, enlightenment and physical well-being, you would not hesitate a second.

You will have an opportunity to take that step-right into a life of happiness and success as you continue through this book. Now it will not be quick and easy. It will not be perfect and it definitely will not be overnight but it is simple. It is the best way we know how to change a person's life and their generation to come.

This book is about sharing with you the best practices about building and maintaining a profitable Referral Marketing Business. The Founders of the $18 Entrepreneur studied the industry and identified the most effective ways of building this unique model. So, let's get started.

CHAPTER 2.

"NETWORK MARKETING ISN'T PERFECT, IT'S JUST BETTER" -Eric Worre

The reason people do not join a Multilevel Marketing business is the fundamental disbelief in the industry or a fundamental disbelief in themselves.

Guidelines for multi-level marketing or Network Marketing, as we often call it, has transformed the dynamics of the profession over the years.

Instead of teaching a "hunter's" mentality where you prospect everybody who can fog up a mirror and immediately get them in front of the company's website that show Big Homes, Fancy Cars and Walking on the beach, there is a new trend.

Network marketing is much more about "branding" the **Team** because the leaders of the team is the attraction.

Most significantly, you have to look for a community of compatible people who are experiencing the success you would like. - Should you surround yourself with entrepreneurs who are succeeding then you will start to mirror their success. Should you constantly plug into what they are teaching and using the things they suggest for you, then you will begin to see your business grow.

Walk like them, talk like them, soon, you will be effective like them! If you are able to copy their success, you will then be the next to become replicated. How great is that?

CHAPTER 3

WHAT NEXT?

Now that you have plunked down that credit card, what do you do next? As absurd as it may seem, there are many people who believe that they simply been handed a meal ticket because they signed up. Being a part of a quick growing Network Marketing business is not a guarantee that you will be effective.

It is simply a chance for you personally to benefit from the momentum the Team can offer. Bear in mind that it takes serious effort to build any type of business, even one inside a fast growing company. In addition, that is why joining the right Team can provide an advantage in creating an effective business.

Let us look at the training. The web is huge and you will find numerous methods for marketing to numerous individuals all over the world. They must have a system in place so your best efforts will not go undetected as well as your business will not FAIL!

CHAPTER 4

THE $18 ENTREPRENEUR ELEPHANT EATING EXPERIENCE:

The fundamental idea for Network Marketing is for those who desire to create their very own financial security. In some instances, the person might want to start Full-Time, in other instances; she or he begins Part-Time and develops the business by working a couple of hours every week. After the earning exceed the current job, she or he will frequently quit the full-time job and transfer their efforts to the self-employment to keep growing the business.

Most people do not like sales, unless you are a professional sales rep. This book describes a method that may help you market your business, because if you cannot get anyone to look at your opportunity then the chances of success are very slim. With that said, it is your business. While you grow and discover, you need to get confident with a system that will give you the best chance to succeed. In the end, you alone have the effect of your ability to succeed!

Being part of a quick growing home business is not a guarantee that you will be effective it is simply a great chance for you personally to benefit from the momentum a quick growing company can offer.

The $18 Entrepreneur

CHAPTER 5

EIGHTEEN STEPS TO ENGAGEMENT~

- Step1: Watch the Introduction Video
- Step2: Download The $18 Entrepreneur e-book
- Step3: Watch company video
- Step4: Set your Goals (the first 18 prospects)
- Step5: Marketing Strategy (Social Media)
- Step6: Post Cards/Flyers/Business Cards
- Step7: Other Advertising
- Step8: Weekly Opportunity Webinars
- Step9: One on One Invitation
- Step10: Private Phone Invitation
- Step11: 3 Way Calls
- Step12: Commit to weekly Training Call
- Step13: Follow up on Engage18 Prospects

- Step 14: Big Events (Always Promote the next)
- Step 15: G.I.F.T. Exchange
- Step 16: Back Office Training
- Step 17: Contact Sponsor or next level leader regularly
- Step 18: Review the Educational Products

Step 1.

Video (https://vimeo.com/226583050)

THE $18 ENTREPRENEURS created a video and this e-book to give you the tools to share this opportunity more effectively. Understanding that it is not the only Road Map to your success. We have found that if you follow the right system you can expect certain success.

Most people fail in Network Marketing for one of two reasons:

> 1. They don't know what to so they do nothing

2. They do the wrong thing, they get rejected and quit

First- they do not know what to do so they do nothing and blame their lack of success to the industry, product and lack of training or their sponsor.

Second- If they do the wrong thing they run off friends, relatives and coworkers. They will ruin a good recruit. Then they quit.

In both cases irrevocable harm is done, they become jaded and never want to do "that" again.

Step 2.

The first two components are the foundation of the model. Once a person has watched the initial Video and has downloaded this ebook, the rest of the plan flows easily around it.

Step 3.

Review the Four Corners Alliance Group website. Once a person has reviewed this in its entirety, they will be ready to engage in the next required steps. If this is not your first time reviewing the website. By reviewing it again, it will reinforce why you made the initial decision.

Step 4.

Set your Goals—

When you ask people to raise their hand if they believe in the power of written goals, every hand will go up. Yet when you ask how many of them have written goals for the month or year, very few hands go up. Research has proven that those who write their goals down accomplish significantly more than those who do not write their goals. With that in mind, we wanted to offer a goal setting primer. Keep them few in numbers -- Write down the first 18 people you want to help change their lives. These should be people who you have a good deal of respect for and they respect you.

Marketing Strategy - are grouped together in that they are the crux of the Formula. This step is crucial in that it is a target practice that encompasses a direct approach rather that a "Shotgun" approach.

Let me explain. Most new recruits write a list and blast everyone on it with "Verbal Vomit". They hit their family and friends with a barrage of information and are surprised when they turn them down. They turn them down for two reasons...

1. You engaged them with too much information and they make a decision based on that. They see you as a novice who is trying to posture yourself as an expert. (They will NEVER consider YOU the expert)
2. They think they will have to do the same thing and they are afraid of everything it represents i.e. Bothering family and friends, speaking in public, learning all the difficult facts and figures

With our targeted Engage 18™ model, you are able to become laser focused and fine-tuned toward a specific and measurable group. Once that target group has been PROPERLY presented to and followed up on thoroughly, we are able to have a quantifiable measurement of success.

The Engage 18™ is simple. Every new $18 Entrepreneur™ is required to create a Slate of 18 potential members. Each person on the slate will be either sent an introduction Postcard, e-mail, text or a phone call. They will see and sense the urgency of the new sponsor wanting them to see the new opportunity they are now a part of.

Once this battery of approach has been completed, the sponsor should be able to schedule a One on One and or a three Way call or a Private Phone Presentation with a Next Level Leader.

These 18 people on the recruit Engage 18™ slate will now do one of two things...

- They will either Sign up and commit to the process
- They will tell you NO.

Most people FEAR the NO. You should look forward to it. NO just means Never Obsess. In other words, you never have to obsess as to whether THAT one is ready. If they tell you NO, Move on.

The next few paragraph will cover some example of scripts for the written media. These can be used through email, text or letter.

STEP 5

First: - Letter

Subject line: Why I thought of you?

Hey, (Friend)

When I jumped on this I immediately thought of you.
It is a business with multiple income streams and
unlimited earning potential, with an incredible
support system.

Now I know you are probably skeptical. I was too at first.
However, I did my due diligence on this and could not wait
to tell you about it.

The 4Corners Alliance Group is all about giving people the financial tools, training and guidance to secure a solid future for themselves and their families.

However, where it gets interesting is that you can spread the word about these products to a huge global marketplace that really needs this now more than ever.

In addition, when you do spread the word, people will come. They already have. The fact is 4Corners is experiencing exponential growth in a very short period of time.

Of course, if you are like me you have probably seen pitches left and right about the "next big thing". I am here to tell you that this really is different.

Are you around this week to talk about it on the phone? I would love to connect and go more in depth about the compensation plan, because once you see that it really becomes a no brainer to get in on this.

Just give me a call at or just reply to this email and we will set up a call. You are going to love this!

Thanks,

(Your Name)

PS – If you want to jump in right now just go to:

http://bit.ly/2vb0ecu (user name) and you can check it all out.

Once I saw what it was all about I was hooked, and I think you will be too!

Second – Email

Subject line: I saw this and thought of you

Hi [first name],

What if you were part of a system that gave you multiple income streams and unlimited earning potential all for less than the cost of a good pizza?

I know that sounds hard to believe, but hear me out, because this is the real deal.

The 4Corners Alliance Group gives you the financial tools, training and guidance you need for

both yourself and the people you bring into the fold.

Moreover, this company is growing faster than anything I have ever seen.

Check it out here:

http://bit.ly/2vb0ecu (user name)

let us set up a time to talk about it and I will explain the generous compensation plan.

Just give me a call at or just reply to this email.

Thanks,

Third- Text—FB/Twitter

Hey (name)

Have you heard how to leverage $18 out of pocket one time?

Watch this: http://bit.ly/2vb0ecu (user name)

Join US!

(Your name)

Step 6

Printed Material.

Postcards/Flyers/Newspaper/Magazine Advertising-

All of these media sources are great. Some can be costly.

Some scripts: *"Is a onetime affordable cost of $18 worth making $500 to $10,000 in 12 months or less? Watch this:*

http://bit.ly/2vb0ecu *(user name) Then call me at: (your number)."*

"Don't underestimate the earning power of an$18 Online Business. Learn how to thrive in the current economy! Watch this:

http://bit.ly/2vb0ecu *(user name)   Then call me at: (your number)."*

"What is an $18 Entrepreneur? A great business that you can have for only $18.00 out of pocket. Watch this:

http://bit.ly/2vb0ecu (user name) Then call me at (your number)

Step 7.

Other Advertising;

Business Cards – should always give a prospect a way to reach you or view your website.

Bulletin Boards at your church, schools, restaurants and any other venue that will allow you to post your business card.

Step 8.

Weekly Opportunity Webinars;

Invite your prospects to attend weekly webinars. Your goal is to have one new prospect on each call.

Step 9

One on One/3 way calls/Phone calls used for inviting a prospect to view a presentation or attend a webinar. These are not to be used via texting or email.

Getting someone to look at your opportunity because if you cannot get someone to take a look then the chances of success is very slim. It is not uncommon for you to invite 10 people to take a look and only get 1. To improve that ratio, you need to have an inviting strategy. There are eight step to an invite that will improve your ratio by eight. We included a couple of examples:** Excerpts taken from "Go *Pro – 7 Steps to becoming a Network Marketing Professional by Eric Worre*"

These are the steps:

1. Be in a Hurry
2. Compliment your prospect
3. Make the invitation
4. If I _____Would you?
5. Get a Time Commitment
6. Confirm
7. Get a Time and Number
8. Get off the Phone

1: Be in a Hurry

This is a psychological issue, people are always more attracted to a person who is busy and has things going on. If you start every call or face-to-face conversation with the feeling that you are in a hurry, you will find your invitations will be shorter, there will be less questions and people will respect you and your time much more.

For warm market prospects: • "I don't have a lot of time to talk, but it was really important I reach you" •

"I'm running out the door, but I needed to talk to you really quick"

For cold market prospects:

• "Now isn't the time to get into this and I have to go, but..."

• "I'm have to run, but..." Get the message?

Set the tone with some urgency

2: Compliment the Prospect

This is critical. The sincere compliment (and it must be sincere) opens the door to real communication and will make the prospect much more agreeable to hearing what you have to say.

For warm market prospects:

"You've been wildly successful and I've always respected the way you've done business."

"You've always been so supportive of me and I appreciate that so much." "You're one of the most connected people I know and I've always admired that about you." "You have an amazing mind for business "I was thinking... who are the sharpest people I know? And I thought of you."

""I need someone to find the holes in something I'm looking at and absolutely nothing gets past you." "

"You're one of the smartest people I know and I really trust your judgment. "

For cold market prospects:

"You've given me/us some of the best service I've/we've ever received." "You are super sharp. Can I ask what you do for a living?"

3: The Invitation.

In this situation, one size does NOT fit all.

Direct Approaches - which you will use when you are talking about an opportunity for THEM specifically.

Indirect Approaches - which you will use to ask for help or advice.

Super Indirect Approaches - which you will use to ask people if they know others who might be interested.

Direct Approach Scripts (and remember, you've already done step 1 and step 2)

For warm market: "I found something you really need to see"

"I'm launching a new business and I really want you to take a look at it"

"Are you still looking for a job (or a different job)? I have found a way for both of us to start a great business without all the risks.

"Let me ask you a question, off the record. If there were a business, you could start working part-time from your home that could replace your full-time income, would that interest you?

"I found an exciting business, and together, I think we could do something special 1+1 might add up to 10."

For cold market: "Have you ever thought of diversifying your income?"

"Do you plan on doing what you're doing now for the rest of your career?" "I have something that might interest you. Now's not the time to get into it but..."

The Indirect Approach is another powerful tool to helping people get past their initial resistance and understand your opportunity. This approach is best used when you are just getting started and it is simply asking people for help or guidance.

For warm market: "I'm thinking about getting started with a business I can run from my home. Would you help me check it out and see if it's for real?"

"I found a business I'm really excited about, but what do I know? You have so much experience. Would you look at it for me if I made it easy and let me know if you think I'm making the right move?"

"A friend told me the best thing I could do when starting a business is to have people I respect take a look at it and give me some guidance. Would you be willing to do that for me if I made it simple?"

For cold market:

Direct and Super Indirect work best for cold market.

Super-Indirect Scripts Super-Indirect Approaches are incredibly powerful and play on a number of psychological levels. "The business I'm in clearly isn't for you, but I wanted to ask, who do you know that is ambitious, money motivated and would be excited about the idea of adding more cash flow to their lives?"

"Who do you know that might be looking for a strong business they could run from their home?

"I work with a company that's expanding in our area and I'm looking for some sharp people that might be interested in some additional cash flow. Do you know anyone who might fit that description?"

In most cases, they're going to ask you for more information before they give you any names (behind that request with be curiosity and intrigue thinking this might be for them... but they're not going to admit that to you yet). When they ask you for more information first, just respond like this. "That makes sense. You'll want to know about it before you refer some of your contacts" Then just move to step 4 for cold market:

Cold market is exactly the same as warm market for Super Indirect. Just use the scripts above or any variation that is comfortable for you.

4: If I gave you _____Would You Watch it, read it or Listen to it?

You are not going to offer your third party tool, unless they agree to do something in return.

> "IF I gave you a link to an online presentation that explained everything, WOULD YOU click on it and watch it?

" If you have done the first three steps properly, the answer will be yes.

If they ask for more information first, just respond with "I understand that you want more information, but all of what you're looking for is on the Link. The fastest way for you to really understand what I am talking about will be to review that material.

So, if I gave it to you, would you review it?" If they say no, they will not review it then thank them for their time and move on. In addition, review steps 1-3 to see what you could have done better.

Do NOT give them your material!

5: Time Commitment

"When do you think you could watch the link for sure?" Do not suggest a time for them. Ask the question and have them give you the time. If it is not definitive "I'll try to do it sometime", then tell them. "I don't want to waste your time or mine. Why don't we just try to lock in a time you'll have seen it for sure?" The key is to get them to say YES a second time. Saying yes to step four is NOT a commitment.

6: Confirmation

If they say, they will watch the link on Thursday night your response should be: "So, if I called you on Friday, you'll have watched it for sure right?

" The key to step six is they have now said three times that they will follow through and they have done it all by themselves. They have set a real appointment with you for the future.

Step 9:

Time and Number

"What's the best number and time for me to call?" Now they have said yes 4 times and the chances they will follow through has been increased from less than 10% to over 80%. Note: Please put this appointment in a place you will not forget.

Step 10:

Get off the Phone...

Remember, you are in a hurry right?

The best thing is to say something like "Great. We'll talk then. Gotta run!"

So those are the eight steps with some of the hottest scripts in MLM on what to say.

Step 11:

Commit to Weekly Training call- -

1- Be on the calls

2- Have you people on the calls

3- Contribute to the calls

Commit to a take away from each call that you can discuss with your team the next day.

Step 12:

Follow up

Follow up on Engage 18 Prospects (the 1st 18 prospects on your list).

1. Reach out to them daily
2. Partner with a business partner to give them a call

Step. 13:

Big Events

1. Always promote to the next big event

2. Have contest to qualify for the next Big Event

Step. 14:

G.I.F.T. Exchange

(Give It Forward Today)

1. Review the Pay It Forward strategies: *** see link at the end of book.

Step 15:

Back Office Training

1. Review your back office
2. Watch the company training video
3. Review the FAQ section
4. Attend weekly training call
5. Request training on back office from your sponsor

Step 16:

Contact Next Level Leader Regularly

1. They are your support and business partner
2. Call or meet weekly

Step 17:

Review the Educational Products.

1. Review the E-books for each level
2. Understand how they can benefit you/your family and your customers.

Step 18:

Have FUN!

When you treat your business like a fun event it becomes a labor of LOVE. Remember to enjoy yourself always.

CHAPTER 6

FIRST SPONSORED PARTNER—*WHAT DO I DO?*

1. *Welcome Letter- -*

Hello:

Welcome to the 4 Corners Power Team! You are now part of a rapidly growing community of success driven and profit minded entrepreneurs focused on building and nurturing a team of highly motivated enterprising people.

You will be connected to the 4Corners contact list and email system, which means that you will stay in the loop on all upcoming events, promotions, product rollouts and marketing initiatives as they happen. Here are 4 ways that 4Corners is different from anything you may have experienced in the past:

1. You now have a robust suite of financial products that will give its users a competitive edge in the marketplace.

2. You now have an EXPLOSIVE wealth opportunity and a safe and secure worldwide money in and money out option. This means, weekly payouts that happen literally while you sleep.

3. You now have access to an elite support system of technical, marketing and customer service experts whose primary focus is YOUR success.

4. You now have HUGE growth potential that can begin immediately. Yes, this is truly an exciting time to be a part of the 4Corners business model, with the fulfillment of all your financial goals on the horizon.

Let's Get Started: **FIRST 2 Days**

1. Review the marketing and compensation plan so you can hit the ground running.

2. Make a List of the first 18 people you will ask to look at your business. Contact within 24 hours

3. Get your own landing page (you can order it through your back office).

4. Get your own Domain, used to direct prospects to landing page.

5. Additional Prospecting Process—**below is a one-liner Ad (attach your domain name) and send to All of your phone contact thru text, do the same with email. This is simple and essential for you to do, and everyone else who joins your team, to get off to a fast start.**

6. Join our weekly training and prospecting calls (time and locations to TBA)

7. Join our Facebook page at The 4 Corners POWER Team

8. Share your Goals with your sponsor: This is a good time to budget your time and laying the groundwork for a growth plan that ties in with how much you want to earn and how quickly you want to get there.

9. If you have any questions at all, please do not hesitate to contact your success partners here at the $18 Entrepreneurs.

10. Sample Ad: (**Copy & paste this ad below to every single text, email, and social media contact that you have)...**
11. **Subject Line: Leverage $18!**
12. **Have you heard how you can Leverage $18, one time, out of pocket?**
13. **Watch This!**
14.
15. http://bit.ly/2vb0ecu **(user name)**
16. **Now, Join Our Team! (your join link)**
Your INFO:

Send this letter to all of your New Team members (be sure to change the name). So dive in, explore, and start getting excited about all the possibilities of being a part of 4Corners Power Team and an $18 ENTREPRENEUR!

The $18   ENTREPRENEUR-Have   them duplicate what you did.

CHAPTER 7

REFERENCE MATERIAL

1. Landing Page-- (user name)

2.

PayitForward http://bit.ly/2vb0ecu **Video--**

https://youtu.be/G3U4fOboKA8

3

Conclusion:

The tragedy of life does not lie in not reaching your goals, the tragedy lies in not having any goals to reach. It is not a calamity to die with dreams unfulfilled, but it is a calamity not to dream. It is not a disaster to be unable to capture your ideas, but it is a disaster to have no ideas to capture. It is not a disgrace not to reach the stars but is a disgrace to have no stars to reach. Some people spend all their life on a boring little island called the "someday Isle" someday I'll be happy, someday I'll take that dream vacation, someday I'll build that dream home, someday I'll have that dream car, someday I'll be able to help other. Life is not a dress rehearsal. Life is here and it is now. We have the vehicle to get off that 'someday island" Use it! You are an $18 ENTREPRENEUR.

www.ingramcontent.com/pod-product-compliance
Lightning Source LLC
Chambersburg PA
CBHW061223180526
45170CB00003B/1135